MAKE
BAKE
GROW
& SEW

ISBN (HB)0 00 195255-2

CIP data available from The British Library

First published by William Collins Sons & Co Ltd 1989

Text © Judy Hindley & Judy Bastyra 1989

Illustrations © William Collins Sons & Co Ltd 1989

Printed in Great Britain by
The Eagle Press Plc, Glasgow

MAKE
BAKE
GROW
& SEW

Written by

Judy Hindley and Judy Bastyra

Illustrated by

Pauline King

Collins

CONTENTS

ABOUT THIS BOOK

Did you know that a pip from an orange or an apple can grow into a little tree? Or that you can make butter just by shaking milk for a long time; or make a musical instrument from a piece of wood and elastic bands?

This book shows you how to do all these things and lots more besides. There are four different sections: Baking, Growing, Sewing and Making, all full of interesting and fun ideas.

BAKING

Find out how to make all sorts of delicious food and drink - from ice cream and milk shakes to a complete meal for your supper. There are plenty of recipes and ideas for food that you can make without even using an oven, such as salads, dips and sandwiches.

SEWING

This section shows you all the things you need in a sewing kit. It gives ideas on simple things to make for yourself or as presents for friends, such as bags, pillows and cushions. You can also find out how to stitch pictures and designs on material.

GROWING

Here you can find out how to plan and look after a garden. There are tips on the best plants to grow and how to grow them, along with a guide to garden creatures and a handy list of gardener's terms.

MAKING

Set up your very own workshop and find out how to turn ordinary objects into exciting things to give as presents or keep. There is a beautiful desk top set to make, ideas for fancy dress and lots more too.

Be Safe

It is a good idea to check first to see if you might need an adult to help you with the ideas in this book, especially if you are going to be using an oven or sharp things such as knives or scissors.

Hints and Tips

There is a list of handy hints and safety tips on pages 62-63.

Exploring an egg

A hard-boiled egg is a very useful thing. It can be a picnic lunch in its own container. It can be mashed and mixed with mayonnaise for a delicious sandwich. You can paint it and colour it and do magic tricks with it.

A soft-boiled egg is a cosy lunch or supper. You can make a hat for it to keep it warm while you lay the table.

But a raw egg really is amazing. The yolk has a delicate sac. The 'white' is clear and gluey. The yolk swings in the white, protected by the shell.

Brown Meringues

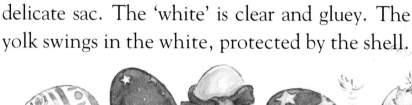

You will need:

1 egg white (room temperature)

Pinch of Salt

4 tablespoons Demerara sugar

You will also need:
a mixing bowl and a baking sheet, greaseproof paper (or brown paper), a rotary whisk, a teaspoon and oven gloves.

1 Have someone turn on the oven to Gas Mark 1 (140°C/275°F). You must have a very cool oven or the meringues will burn.

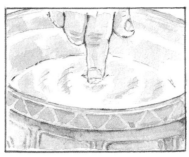

2 Test to check that the white is at room temperature by dipping your finger in it. The temperature is correct if you can't feel the egg.

3 Whisk the egg white and salt in a bowl. It will get bubbly. The bubbles get smaller and thicker until the mixture stands in peaks.

4 Sprinkle the sugar on the mixture, whisking after each spoonful. Keep whisking until the mixture is stiff again.

5 Put spoonfuls of this mixture on a sheet of greaseproof paper on a baking sheet. Bake for 2 hours.

6 Using oven gloves on both hands, take out the baking sheet and let it cool. Then peel the meringues from the paper.

Cracking an egg

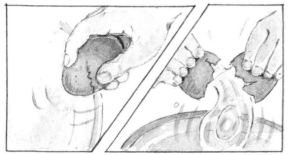

Give it a good sharp tap on the side of a cup or bowl (one with a thinnish rim works best). Pull the two halves apart and let the egg gently slide out. Now you can see what's inside.

Separating an egg

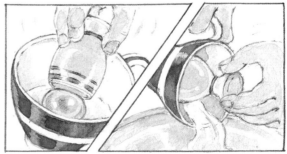

Put an egg cup over the yolk and pour the white into another bowl or cup. You can easily scoop up little bits of broken shell with a big piece of shell. The shell cuts through the white – a spoon won't do this.

Milk shakes and butter-making

A tall, cool glass of milk is a wonderful thing to drink on a warm day. To make it special, mix it with chocolate, ice cream or fruit. Whisk it until it's full of foamy bubbles – and drink it right away while it's still bubbly.

If you whisk milk or shake it in a jar until it's light and foamy – you have a milk shake. But if you shake and shake and shake and shake – you have butter! (That's how butter is made.)

Whisking practice

Some whisks are a little difficult to get the hang of. Practise by putting a few good squirts of washing-up liquid in a plastic bowl – you can make great castles of foam.

Foamy chocolate milk

Have you ever tried mixing cocoa with milk or cold water? It just won't work. If you first mix the cocoa with some sugar – Presto! it mixes easily.

For each person, you need:

1 teaspoon of cocoa
2 teaspoons of sugar
1 cup of milk
about a tablespoon of water
You also need:
spoons to measure,
a whisk, a glass and
a mixing bowl. (Use a bowl
with a lip if you can.)

Mix the cocoa and sugar in the bowl. Add the water and mix it thoroughly. Stir in the milk. Now whisk it until it's frothy, pour it into the glass and drink it up.

The story of milk and butter

The sun grows the grass. The grass feeds the cow. The cow makes the milk. The farmer takes the milk.

A truck takes it from the farm to the dairy.

The dairy skims the cream, the cream is churned and churned. And out comes butter – the colour of the sun.

Butter-making

When cream (or creamy milk) is churned or shaken, the tiny drops of butterfat begin to stick together. The tiny drops make bigger drops, the drops make little lumps, the lumps make a pat of butter. You can see for yourself if you are patient. Use cream if you can because it has more butterfat.

Put it in a clean, screwtop jar, about ⅓ full, with about ¼ teaspoon of salt.

Then just shake and shake. It can take a long time – perhaps 20 minutes. After a while, look for a floating pat of butter. Drain it on a paper towel – and then you can spread it on bread.

Thick raspberry milk shake

Thick milk shakes are made with soft ice cream. (You can flavour them with fruit, cocoa or honey, too.)

For each person, you need:
a cupful of fresh or frozen raspberries, or a small tin (about 75g drained)
2 teaspoons of sugar
1 cup of milk
2 heaped tablespoons of soft vanilla ice cream
You will also need:
a bowl, a big wooden mixing spoon and a rotary whisk

Mix the raspberries and sugar in the bowl until the fruit is soft and slushy. Use the back of the spoon. Mix in the milk and ice cream. Then whisk it up until it's thick and frothy.

rotary whisk

spring whisk

9

Ice cream and lollies

Have you ever seen a puddle turn to ice in the winter?
The ice starts like a skin, then it freezes deeper and
deeper as tiny, invisible crystals lock together.
When you make ice cream, you have to
stir it up to break up the crystals.
That is what makes it creamy.

Home-made ice lollies

For containers, you can use:

a plastic egg carton   *an ice tray*   *ice lolly moulds*

Good things to freeze are:

apple juice

fruit yoghurts

orange juice   *chocolate milk*   *blackcurrant juice*

1 Pour the liquid you have
chosen into the containers.
Leave some space at the top
of each container as liquids
swell when they freeze.

2 For handles, you can stick
cocktail sticks into small
pieces of grape, or cherry.
Then they will stand
upright.

*Put the full
containers into the
ice-making
compartment of a
fridge.*

3 When the lollies are
frozen, run some hot water
over the bottom of the
containers to loosen them.
Then you can take them out.

Home-made ice cream

What you need:

200g soft fruit

lots of ice cubes

a mixing bowl

a large biscuit tin

100g caster sugar

300ml double cream

a wooden spoon

some salt

a fork

a squeeze of lemon juice

a tea towel

*a smaller tin with
a tight-fitting lid*

1 Mash the fruit and sugar with the fork until soft and pulpy. Add the lemon juice and the cream. Mix them all together.

2 Put a layer of ice cubes, then a layer of salt at the bottom of the large tin. Put the smaller tin on top. Add more layers of ice cubes and salt.

3 Pour the mixture into the smaller tin and put the lid on. Then wrap the tea towel around the large tin and leave for 30 minutes.

4 Remove the tea towel and lid. Use the wooden spoon to scrape the mixture from the sides of the tin, to keep it from freezing solid.

5 Be sure that you put the lid back on carefully. Cover the tin again with the tea towel and leave for another 10 minutes.

6 Remove the tea towel and lid. Stir the mixture again until it is thick and smooth. Scoop it out and pile it into bowls.

Baked chocolate sauce
For 4 people you need:

2 large Mars bars, cut into pieces

4 tablespoons of water

1 teaspoon of instant coffee

an ovenproof dish

a wooden spoon

some oven gloves

a jug for serving (not a glass one)

Ask an adult to help you make this.

1 Turn on the oven to Gas Mark 4 (180°C/350°F).

2 Put the Mars bar pieces, instant coffee and water into the ovenproof dish. Put it in the oven for about 6 minutes, until it is melted.

3 Take the dish out of the oven. Set it down on something that won't burn. Stir the mixture with the wooden spoon until it is smooth and thick. Pour it into the serving jug.

4 Pour it over the ice cream while it is still warm.

11

Dips and salads

broad beans

spring onions

radishes

mushrooms

You can eat little radishes and carrots
straight from the garden –
all they really need is a good scrub
and maybe a pinch of salt.
What other raw vegetables have you tried?
Spinach? Cabbage? French beans?
Cauliflower?
There are so many ways to make them tempting.
Wash them carefully,
trim away the rough bits,
and try some experiments.

celery

carrots

tomatoes

kidney beans

broccoli

peas

beetroot

cucumber

Drying lettuce leaves   **Slicing vegetables**   **Grating vegetables**

You can dry lettuce leaves
without bruising them if you
wrap them in a clean, dry
tea towel and spin it around.
The water flies off the leaves
into the tea towel.

Use a serrated knife.
Hold the vegetable firmly on
a chopping board with one
hand and slice with the
other. Some have wonderful
patterns inside – stars and
rings of different colours.

Always push away from
yourself and keep going in
the same direction. Don't try
to grate the bit you're
holding onto – just eat it up.
Vegetables sharpen your
appetite.

French dressing

This is good on any combination of vegetables – sliced or grated, tossed together or arranged on a plate.

Put into a clean screwtop jar –
1 teaspoon brown sugar,
½ teaspoon mustard,
salt and pepper,
4 tablespoons oil,
1 tablespoon vinegar,
1 tablespoon lemon juice.

Screw the lid on tightly. Shake it until it's a mass of tiny honey-coloured bubbles.

Pink dip

Stir in a little bowl –
4 tablespoons thick mayonnaise,
2 tablespoons tomato ketchup.
You can add chopped herbs. Thin with a little vinegar to make a dressing.

Cheesy dip

Stir in a little bowl –
4 tablespoons cream cheese,
2 tablespoons sour cream or natural yoghurt,
1 teaspoon chopped chives,
salt and pepper.

Creamy potato salad

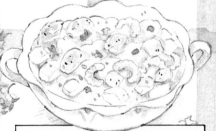

Slice and put in a bowl –
500g cooked new potatoes,
2 celery sticks,
1 spring onion,
2 gherkins,
a handful of chopped parsley.
Mix together and stir into the vegetables –
3 tablespoons thick mayonnaise,
2 tablespoons natural yoghurt
a little salt and pepper.

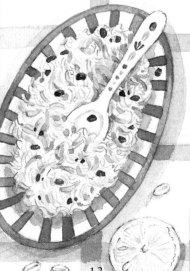

Carrot salad

Grate in a bowl –
6 medium carrots, 1 apple.
Mix in with a fork –
2 tablespoons raisins
or desiccated coconut or dry roasted peanuts,
2 tablespoons lemon juice,
3 tablespoons orange juice,
salt and pepper.

Party sandwiches

When you make beautiful sandwiches for a party, cover them with cling film or with foil until the party begins. Then they will taste as good as they look.

Salad fillings

Thin buttered bread is delicious with slices of tomato or thin slices of cucumber, or some watercress. Just give it a sprinkle of salt and pepper. Or try mixing salads with: a thick layer of cream cheese, yellow cheese, grated to bring out the flavour, egg mayonnaise, or slices of hard-boiled egg.

Egg mayonnaise

To serve 3 people, you will need:-
2 hard-boiled eggs (shelled)
a knob of soft butter
1 tablespoon of mayonnaise
salt and pepper
You also need a small mixing bowl and a fork to mash the eggs.

Mash the eggs in the bowl until they are crumbly. Mix in the butter and then the mayonnaise, salt and pepper.
To make it pink, add a teaspoon of tomato ketchup

Cottage cheese fillings

A small carton of cottage cheese (100g) is enough for 3 or 4 people. Try it with one of these –

1 tablespoon of chopped cooked chicken with salt and pepper

1 tablespoon of finely chopped ham, with a small, chopped tomato and salt and pepper.

Cream cheese fillings

Cream cheese is easier to spread if you take it out of the fridge an hour or so before you need it. To soften it, press the cream cheese against the inside of the bowl with the back of a big spoon. A small carton (100g) is enough for 3 or 4 people. Good things to mix into it are –
chopped black olives, mashed ripe banana, chopped fruit, such as apple, dates or pineapple.

Sweet fillings

Honey, jam, marmalade or lemon curd are particularly good on wholemeal bread, with just a scrape of butter or margarine.

Or make your own combinations of fillings – try peanut butter with jam.

To cut little round things like olives and radishes, first slice off a tiny piece to make a flat side. Then it will lie still while you slice it. Always hold firmly and slice downwards.

Monsters

Use little rolls. Cut them almost all the way through the middle. Carefully spread the inside with butter or margarine or a savoury filling. Add a rolled up slice of ham or other cold meat (or cheese) for the sticky-out tongue. Use cocktail sticks to fix on the bits of the face. Remember to take out the cocktail sticks before you bite into them!

Monsters

chopped mustard and cress for hair
olive slices for eyes
carrot sticks or gherkin for nose
slice of radish for mouth

Chequerboard
brown and white bread sandwiches,
cut into fours

15

Patchwork quilt
pink egg mayonnaise
plain egg mayonnaise
cream cheese with olives

Christmas baking

The secret of baking is careful measuring –
thorough mixing – and watching the clock
while the cookies are cooking. Then you can
ice them in all sorts of patterns and colours.

Cookie cut-outs

You will need:

2 eggs

8 heaped tablespoons of sugar

1 level teaspoon bicarbonate of
soda dissolved in 1 tablespoon of
warm water

Mixed in a bowl –
19 heaped tablespoons of plain
flour
2 heaped tablespoons of cut mixed
peel
¼ level teaspoon ground cloves
¼ level teaspoon ground ginger
1 level teaspoon ground cinnamon
a pinch of pepper

You also need:

a mixing bowl

a wooden spoon

a table knife

a whisk

a rolling pin

cooking oil to grease the baking
sheet

oven gloves

several
little bowls

a baking sheet

measuring
spoons

**To ice and decorate, you
need:**

125gms of soft butter or margarine

250gms of icing sugar

currants   coconut

silver balls

chocolate vermicelli

sugar flowers

To colour and flavour –
powdered coffee or chocolate,
or a little juice from tinned or
frozen berries

You may need two hands to stir!

1 Get someone to heat the oven to Gas Mark 4 (180°C/ 350°F). Rub some cooking oil over the baking sheet.

2 Gather everything together and carefully measure out what you need. Beat the eggs and sugar together.

3 Tip the flour mixture into the bowl, little by little. Add the soda water and stir again. Cover the dough and chill it for 30 minutes.

Use oven gloves.

4 Sprinkle flour on a clean surface and on a rolling pin. Roll out the dough, always rolling away from yourself.

5 When it's about 0.6cm thick, you can cut out shapes. Lift them with a knife and place them on a baking sheet.

6 Bake in the oven for 10 minutes. Then take them out of the oven. Slide the knife under each cookie to lift off the sheet.

To ice and decorate

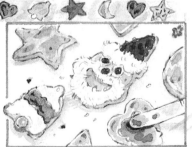

1 Mix the butter, sugar and flavouring in a bowl.

2 If you put the mixture in several little bowls, you can have different tints or colours – pink, dark pink and white for instance.

3 You can create all sorts of special Christmas effects using the icing and some of the decorations shown on the opposite page.

Spices and cinnamon toast

Vanilla is a pod.

Turmeric is what makes curry powder yellow.

How many kinds of spice can you find in your kitchen cupboard? Do you see little jars or boxes with these names?

Spices and flavourings are the perfumes of our food. Look, and sniff, and find which ones you like.

Have you ever looked very closely at a peppercorn? It's really a dried-up berry. A clove is a small, dried flower-bud from a tree and cinnamon is the bark of another tree. Spices usually come in small containers – pounded to powder or ground into little grains so we can measure carefully and sprinkle lightly.

Ginger is a root.

chillies

Good cooks like to experiment with spices. Try a little nutmeg on mashed potato or turnip or cauliflower.

Try a sprinkle of paprika on anything light-coloured – egg salad, tuna fish, or cream cheese on celery.

garlic

cumin seeds

The Chinese word for cloves means "fragrant nails".

cumin seeds chillies turmeric
nutmeg   coriander
cardamom   curry
ginger

Cinnamon toast

Try some buttery, sugary, crunchy cinnamon toast when you come in from the cold.

Mix half a teaspoon of ground cinnamon and three heaped tablespoons of sugar to spread on fresh, hot buttered toast. Keep some in a shaker jar ready to use.

A clean, dry salt shaker is good for sprinkling.

Try a dash of cinnamon on your cocoa – it tastes delicious.

Pomanders

A pomander is not to eat but just to sniff and make your clothes smell wonderful. Stick cloves all over a small orange or apple. (They preserve the fruit.)

Leave space to tie a ribbon round and hang it in your wardrobe.

Planning a picnic

What do you think makes the best sort of
picnic? Do you like fields to run about in?
Do you like rivers to fish for trout in?
Do you like waves that tickle your toes –
or watching a butterfly nose to nose?
Do you like staying outside all day till it's
time to wish on the evening star?
Take something to eat and something to
drink and a blanket to lie on to look at the sky?
Even if you're not far from home, you
can pretend you are...

Here is how to have a wonderful picnic:

Before you start, make a
plan. Early in the morning
(or even the night before),
think of what you'll want to
do and what you'll need. You
might want to make a list to
remind yourself. Here are
some ideas:

For lunch

Chicken drumsticks are good (particularly if you bake them
yourself) or big, hearty sandwiches. Wrap them in cling film
or small plastic bags so they won't dry out. If you want salad
in them, wrap it separately and add it when you get there.
(Otherwise the sandwiches will get damp and squashy.)

If you take hard-boiled eggs, remember the salt. You can wrap it in a small plastic bag with a rubber band around it. Or you can take some in a salt shaker and stop the holes with a strip of sticky tape until you're ready to use it.

Little carrots or radishes from your garden are good to nibble on. If you take tomatoes, pack them on top so they won't get squashed.

Juice or lemonade are the best things to drink. Carry your drink in a thermos or a screwtop jar (ice cubes will help keep it cool).

For later

It's a good idea to save a treat for later...perhaps an apple or orange and a handful of nuts and raisins (kept in a plastic bag with a rubber band around it).

For fun

This is where you have to plan carefully. Remember – the less you take, the less you have to carry home. But you might want some of these: a ball for ball games; a collecting-bag for finding shells or feathers, interesting stones or seeds; some string for fishing (to tie round the jar you brought your drink in).

More things to take on a picnic

A notepad and pencil for drawing
and noting down the things
you find – or writing messages
for a treasure hunt.
Swimming things and a towel
if you're near water.
A damp flannel in a plastic bag –
it feels good to be able to wipe
your sticky hands.

Here are some ideas on things to do:

Make boats out of leaves
and twigs and race them in
a pool or puddle. Decide
what the winning post is,
lie down flat and blow your
boat towards it.

Lie on your back and see
how many shapes you can
find in a cloud.

Make a village of little huts
from mud and twigs, or
smooth flat stones.

Make a necklace with
melon seeds, daisies or
dandelions.

Go ponding with a jam-jar; tie string around it so you can easily pull it out. Dip it into the water to see what lives there. Look hard – some creatures are very small. Can you see anything moving?

If you put in a pellet of bread or cheese, and lie the jar on its side, tadpoles or minnows might swim right inside it.

When you leave, collect all the things you bought. Find the jars and balls and salt shakers.

Be sure to pick up any plastic bags or wrappers.

Before you go, remember what a good time you've just had. Look to see if there's something to make a wish on. You can wish on a new moon, if you spot it over your left shoulder. Or you can say this, to the first star in the sky:

Star light,
Star bright,
First star I see at night,
I wish I may,
I wish I might,
Have the wish I wish tonight...

(What will you wish for now?)

Cooking your own supper

The best part of cooking is sniffing and tasting. See what there is to cook and then find a seasoning...
Are there any fresh herbs in your garden or window box? Are there any dried herbs tucked away in the kitchen cupboard? See if you have any with these names. Sniff them and find out which ones you like. Some of them may seem a little strange... others may remind you of things to eat. Choose one herb to flavour your meat or fish dish. Choose another to make herb butter for your bread.

mint

basil

oregano

chives

dill

sage

rosemary

thyme

parsley

tarragon

garlic

Getting ready to cook

First, check the clock and see if it's time to start. Then ask someone to turn on the oven to Gas Mark 4 (180°C/350°F). Wash your hands and gather the things you need.

For 6 o'clock supper:

4.50 p.m.	get ready
5.00 p.m.	start potato
5.15 p.m.	start meat
5.30 p.m.	start fish and bread
6.00 p.m.	supper is ready

Each person will need:

a small, well-scrubbed potato, with no eyes

a piece of fish fillet, chicken or lamb chop, just big enough for one

two slices of bread, or a large slice cut in half

lemon juice if you're having fish

a banana for pudding

salt, pepper, herbs

butter or margarine

You will also need:

a fork, a knife, a wooden spoon and a small bowl, a baking sheet and baking foil, oven gloves for both hands

The potato may explode if you don't prick it first.

For fish, add a knob of butter and a squeeze of lemon juice.

Remember, if you are having meat, put it in 15 minutes before the bread and fish.

1 Prick the potato very hard, in three places, with a fork. This is important! Put it on the top rack of the oven, where it's hottest.

2 Mix a sprinkling of herbs with a large spoonful of butter and stir till it's soft.

3 Take a piece of foil big enough to wrap round the meat or fish with a little left over. Take another piece for the bread.

4 Put your fish or meat on the foil. Sprinkle with salt, pepper and herbs. Fold the foil to make a little parcel.

5 Spread the herb butter between the slices of bread; wrap them in foil.

6 Check the time. Put the parcels on the baking sheet in the oven. When you open the parcels, keep your face away – the steam is hot.

7 Set the table and tidy up to be ready for supper.

25

Hunting for seeds

blackberry

thistle

How many seeds can you find on
an autumn day?
Seeds grow in so many shapes and in so
many ways. Sometimes they
grow packed together in a case
or right in the
centre of a flower. Have you ever seen the
seed ball of a plane tree?
When the seeds are ripe, it turns
into a handful of fluff. The seeds are
ready to fly on tiny parachutes –
just like a thistle or a dandelion.

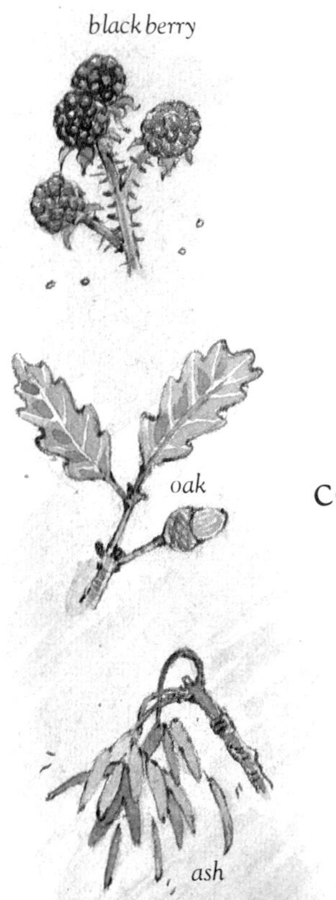

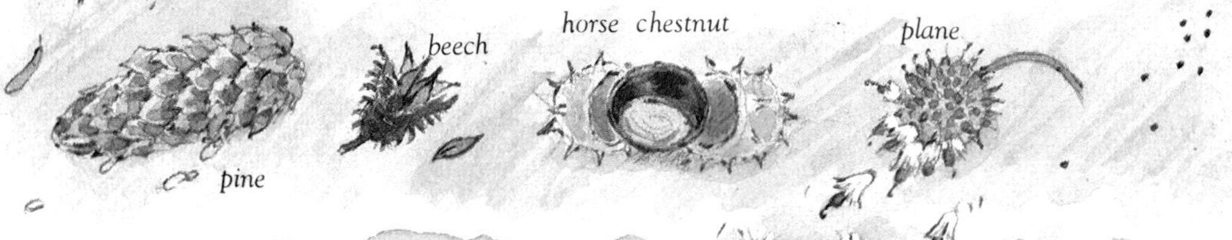

dandelion

oak

poppy

ash

beech

horse chestnut

plane

pine

What is a seed?

A seed is what a new
plant grows from.
Seeds have to get
away from their
parent plant so that
they will have
enough sun and
space to grow in.

Some seeds are big and some are very tiny.

*Seeds have lots of different
ways of getting around.
Some of them glide or spin
in the air or float on water.*

Birds scatter the seeds of fruit they eat – mice and squirrels take seeds away and bury them.

Some seeds have hooks or prickles to hitch a ride on people or animals.

Here is what you can do with seeds that you collect:

Count them and trade them, or play games with them.

Put them in rows. Paint them or make things with them.

Or plant them. They'll grow inside, too, if you plant them in a warm, light and airy spot. They'll think it's spring!

A seed race

Did you know that all of these are seeds? Even a peanut or a coffee bean might grow into a plant or a little tree if it has not been roasted. See how many you can find around your house and have a race to see which grows the fastest.

Inside a seed

Some seeds will grow on a damp flannel or cotton wool or blotting paper. You can watch them sprout.

A seed always has a tough case to protect it. Inside is food for the baby plant, and a live bit called a germ. The germ grows a root and a shoot.

When a seed begins to grow the root starts first (to make sure there's water for the plant).

You can hold a seed in a glass with a wad of cotton wool right next to the side, so you can see how it grows.

Growing seeds

Very hard pips and stones (such as avocado stones) should be soaked for a day in warmish water before you plant them.

Grow date stones and peanuts on a sunny window-sill or near a radiator.

Grow other seeds where it's cool. Remember to keep them in the dark.

Containers

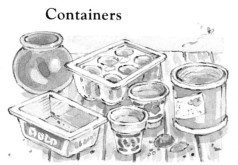

You can start them in all sorts of containers. When the plants have four or five green leaves, you can put them in pots.

Pips and seeds

Cover the seeds with a layer of soil as thick as the seed.

Bean in a jar

You can watch the root and shoot start to grow.

Keep a bean in the bottom of a jar, covered with a little water. Pour the water in carefully.

Potting the seedlings

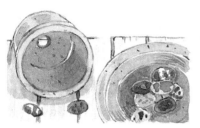

1 Get a pot with a hole at the bottom or a layer of pebbles to let water drain through.

2 Make a good-sized hole in the potting earth.

3 Lift the little plant gently. Let its roots spread out in its new home. Press down the soil around it to hold it firm. Water it.

Mustard and cress

You can use wet cotton wool in an orange skin with a felt-tip funny-face. It will grow green hair!

cotton wool

1 Sow the cress first and the mustard three days later. Scatter the seeds thinly. Keep them damp.

2 Cover with paper or a lid until the shoots grow. You can harvest them with a little pair of scissors when they are 7.5cm tall.

Finding a garden

Wherever plants can grow can be a garden. It can be as big as a park or as small as an eggshell or an old cracked cup on a windowsill. Plants can climb upstairs or hang down from the ceiling...

Look to see where you can have a garden. Is there a good, light corner where some pots will fit? Make sure it isn't near a radiator – that's too hot. Watch out for draughts. Remember that soft light is better than bright sunlight.

If you have a plot outside it should be sunny and protected from the wind. The soil should be crumbly. It's difficult for plants to push through soggy earth that feels like clay.

A very few plants (like moss and ferns) prefer dark, damp corners where nothing else will grow. But most plants need good soil and light and air.

Look at other people's gardens and see what's growing. A plant that grows happily in the soil next door will probably grow healthy and strong for you. Ask your neighbours for some good ideas. They might give you some little plants or roots or cuttings. Gardeners like to share.

Geraniums grow happily in pots, and in hanging baskets suspended from a trellis.

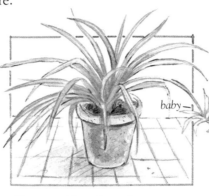

baby —

Pieces of fragrant leaf geranium grow into new ones. Stand them in water until the roots grow. Then plant in pots.

Some spider plants have babies. You can snip one off and start a new plant.

Plants always grow towards the sunlight. Turn your pots now and then so that the plants grow straight.

Little pots of chives, parsley, basil and thyme make an indoor herb garden.

Cress can grow in a butter or margarine tub, or even in an eggshell or an empty orange half.

You can grow a little fruit tree in a dustbin. Since its roots can't spread, it will never get too big.

Planning your garden

Early in spring you can begin to plan.
Remember that most plants need a
sunny, sheltered spot.
The earth should be rich and crumbly.
You can add compost – ask someone to
dig it in.
The ground should be flat so that water
can easily drain.
Is there a spot like this?
What will you plant in it?
It's nice to have something for show,
something for picking, something to eat
and something that smells
delicious…

Buying seeds

Buy your seeds early before
the shops sell out. You and
a friend can share the
packets and you'll each
have twice as many kinds!

32

When to sow

On the packet, it will say just when to sow.

Mark your calendar and sow your seeds early enough to have plenty of growing time in the summer sun.

The packet will also tell you just how far apart the seeds should be.

Here are some handy gardener's words you find on seed packets:

A **drill** is a little groove in the earth where you sow a row of seeds.

A **perennial** is a plant that grows again each year.

A **hardy** plant won't be hurt by frost.

Broadcast is when you scatter the seeds.

An **annual** is a plant you have to sow again each year.

A **half-hardy** plant should not be planted out until the danger of frost is over.

You can start some plants inside and put them out when they are partly grown. A good trick is to cover

each small seedling with a very clean glass jar turned upside down. The jar keeps the seedling moist.

Plants to grow

radishes

French beans

thyme *sage*

carrots

chives

rosemary

mint

Plants for eating:
Carrots – you can sow more as you pull them.
Radishes – eat a few weeks after sowing.
French beans – grow a crop very quickly.
Plants for flavouring:
Chives, rosemary, sage and thyme have
pretty flowers, and you can use their
leaves for flavouring.
Mint – plant it with its root in a pot or
tin or else it will spread everywhere!

Plants for show

mallow

sunflowers

geraniums

lobelia

1st

Mallow – quickly grows big and important, and flowers all summer. It needs lots of room. Lobelia – makes a deep-blue border.

Sunflowers – grow as high as a wall, and songbirds come for the seeds. (You can eat them too.)

Geraniums are very easy to grow from cuttings or seeds and flower for most of the year. They grow happily in pots or in hanging baskets.

Alyssum – spreads like a white carpet and brings honey bees.

Nasturtium – grows almost anywhere; climbs and trails if you want it to. Dwarf varieties are small and compact.

Marigolds – make a golden splash and you can eat the flowers and leaves in salads.

Plants for climbing

Morning Glory – may be a little difficult to start but can grow up to 3m tall.

Honeysuckle – little honey-coloured trumpets which have a beautiful smell.

Ivy – many different kinds grow beautifully from cuttings. Ask your neighbours for some.

Plants for pots

Busy Lizzie – grows very fast and easily from cuttings, and comes in many colours.

African Violet – new plants grow from a leaf in water.

Pot Marigolds and the butterfly flower – especially easy to grow.

Garden tips

Plants grow quickly in warm summer weather.
Check your garden every couple of days. Watch
the shoots poke up and the leaves appear and
then the flower buds and swelling seeds.
Check for pests, pull out weeds and water the soil.

When do you need to water?

Plants need lots of water in the summer – they grow fast
and flower then. If the weather has been dry, test the soil.
Dig down about 5 cm. If it's dry all the way, water it.
Use a watering can or a hose with a gentle spray, and give
the earth a good soak. Or dig a furrow next to a row of
plants, and let water run along it from a hose.

Don't forget your pot plants!

They need a drink
about once a week.
Put the pot in a bucket
of water. When it
stops bubbling the soil
is wet enough.

Always water at the end of
the day, so the water can
sink down while the air is
cooler. Remember that the
plants drink underground,
through their little root hairs.

dandelions

How can you tell a flower from a weed?

A weed is just a plant that
grows where you don't want
it to grow, taking food from
the plants you do want.
Learn to know your own
plants as they sprout. When
different looking plants
appear, you'll know they're
weeds. Learn to recognize
common weeds, such as
dandelions, groundsel,
chickweed and couch grass.
It's easy to pull them out if
you act quickly, and get
them when they're small.

groundsel

chickweed

Guarding your plants from pests

Many creatures like to live in a garden. Some are fun to watch, and good to have there. Others will eat your garden for their dinner – they're the pests.

You can trap snails and slugs in a jar buried in the ground, with a little beer or ale. They like it so much that they drown themselves.

Pests can often be stopped if you catch them at the start. Look for caterpillar eggs on the underside of leaves, and rub them off.

When you find snails and slugs, put them in the open, where birds might see them. Thrushes love to eat snails. Have you ever seen one break open a snail shell on a stone?

You can trap many pests by putting out halves of fruit, like this.

Make a tiny door so slugs creep inside.

A hollowed apple traps woodlice.

A hollowed turnip traps millipedes.

An orange or grapefruit half traps slugs.

Friendly creatures

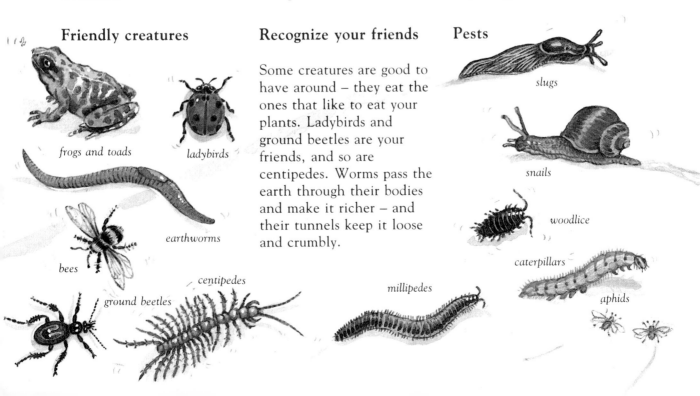

frogs and toads

ladybirds

earthworms

bees

centipedes

ground beetles

Recognize your friends

Some creatures are good to have around – they eat the ones that like to eat your plants. Ladybirds and ground beetles are your friends, and so are centipedes. Worms pass the earth through their bodies and make it richer – and their tunnels keep it loose and crumbly.

Pests

slugs

snails

woodlice

caterpillars

millipedes

aphids

Growing flowers in winter

Did you know you can grow flowers in the winter?
Snowdrops push up through the cold, hard earth.
Sometimes their heads poke up through drifts of snow.
Snowdrops grow from bulbs and so do daffodils,
narcissi, freesias and hyacinths.
They are all quite easy to grow indoors.
You can fool them and make them think
it's nearly spring.
Daffodils and hyacinths are easiest.

To grow a flower from a bulb

You will need:

bulbs

bulb fibre

a pot

pebbles

Use a pot with a hole at the bottom or a layer of pebbles, so the water can drain.

1 Soak some bulb fibre for about one hour, until it's good and wet. Squeeze out any extra water.

Half a hyacinth bulb should show but just the nose of a daffodil bulb.

2 Plant the bulbs with their pointy ends pointing up. Leave enough space to grow around each bulb – 2.5cm will do.

3 Put the bulbs somewhere dark and cool such as a shadowed corner of a shed. Keep the bulb fibre damp. Check it and water it.

4 About 8 weeks later, you can move the bowl to a lighter place – but keep it cool and damp and away from sunlight.

5 Now you can take your flower into the light.

How it grows

The little root hairs suck up the water.

The shoot starts to grow.

The fleshy scales of the bulb are used for the flower's food. Gradually they shrivel and wither away.

Making a sewing kit

You can be someone who always knows
where to find a button or thread –
or just the right scrap of cloth.
Here is what you need for a sewing kit:
something to keep your pins in;
something to store your buttons in;
something to stick your needles into;
something to hold your cotton reels;
something to keep it all in;
a bag for wool and trimmings;
a bag for useful scraps;
a measuring tape and scissors.

Sorting through a scrap bag

Find a piece of cloth and hold it to the light. Look at the pattern that the threads make. This is called the weave.

Sometimes there's a fringe when the thread just at the edge is not held tightly – this is called fraying.

Felt is very useful – it doesn't fray at all. It is perfect for making little bags or purses.

Threading a needle

The hole of a needle is called the eye. Hold it to the light or over some white paper so you can see through it when you thread it.

Cut the thread off neatly. Lick it and press it flat between your fingertips. If it frays, cut it and start again.

Knotting the thread

Make a knot with both ends of the thread. Pull the ends together and twist them round your first finger. Gently roll the loop off with your thumb. Hold it between your thumb and middle finger to pull it into a knot.

Needle case

Use shapes or squares of cut-out felt. Pin them together while you stitch them up.

The smaller one holds the needles. The bigger one is the case. It keeps your fingers from being pricked when you pick it up.

fold over

fold over

Rips and buttons

With a few quick stitches you can make
repairs all by yourself.
Have a good look round for
what needs mending.
Practise stitching on cloth that has a
pattern you can follow.
Always knot the thread so that
it won't pull out.
Always poke the needle up and
down again on the same side
of the cloth.

Stitching up a seam

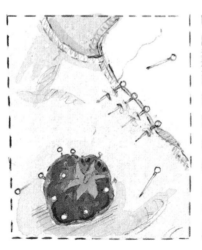
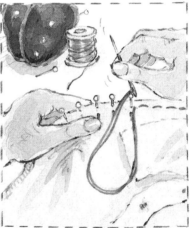

1 Is there a gap in the seam
of your shirt? Look to see
what colour thread the
seam is stitched with and
match it if you can.

2 Hold it together with pins
while you sew it up. Put the
pins in sideways across the
path you plan to stitch
along.

3 You can stitch right over
them and then take all the
pins out when you're
finished.

Sewing on buttons

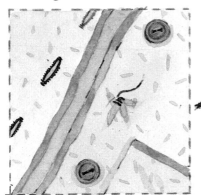 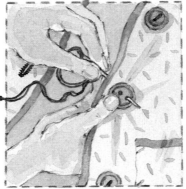 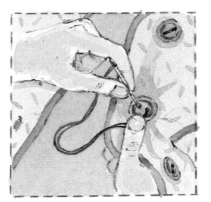

1 First work out where the button goes so it fits through the buttonhole: look for a bit of thread where the old button was.

2 Start from the wrong side of the cloth. Push your needle up through the cloth and then through one of the holes in the button.

3 Push it down through a different hole and through the cloth again. Keep making this stitch until the button is on securely.

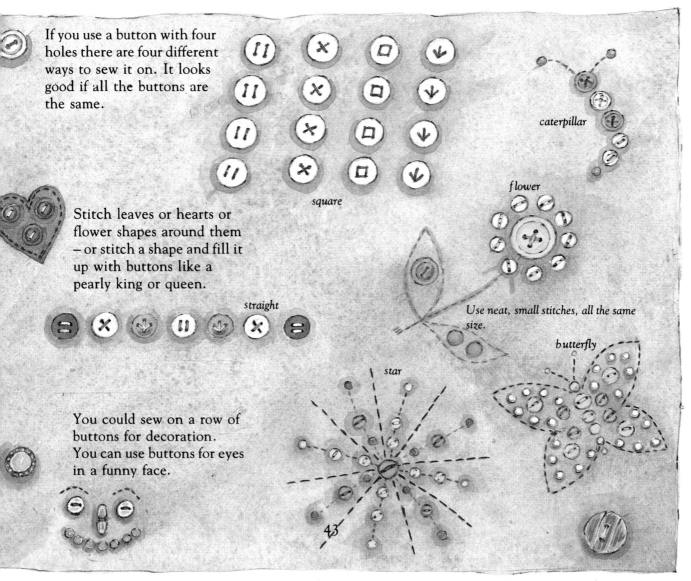

If you use a button with four holes there are four different ways to sew it on. It looks good if all the buttons are the same.

square

caterpillar

Stitch leaves or hearts or flower shapes around them – or stitch a shape and fill it up with buttons like a pearly king or queen.

flower

straight

Use neat, small stitches, all the same size.

butterfly

You could sew on a row of buttons for decoration. You can use buttons for eyes in a funny face.

star

43

Sewing for presents

Embroidery is like drawing with coloured
thread. It turns ordinary things into
special presents.
Embroidery thread is very thick and bright.
Write somebody's name –
or make a heart or flower on:
socks, gloves, scarves,
towels, aprons, napkins,
table mats...

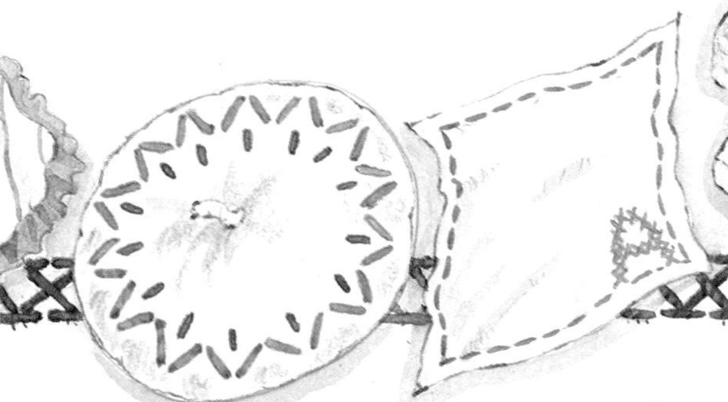

You can make embroidery
stitches with fine wool or
very, very narrow ribbon –
you just need a needle with
a good long eye.

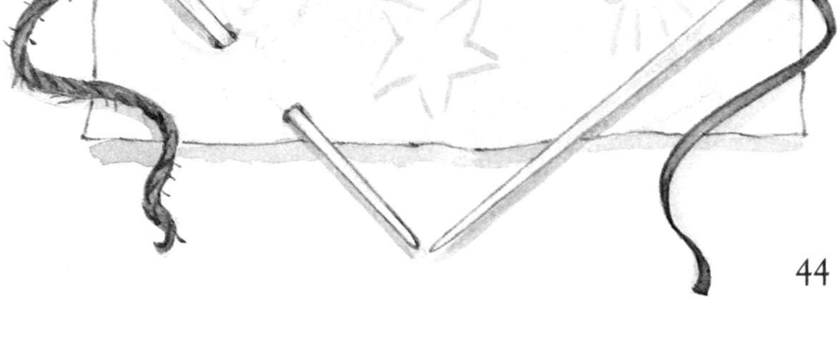

Take care to keep the
stitches neat and regular.
Work out what bits of your
picture to do first. You
might even draw it lightly
on the cloth.

44

Back stitch

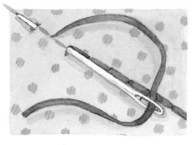

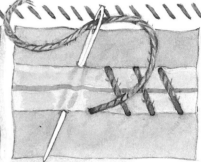

Stitch all the bits in one row before you do the next one.

Back stitch makes a strong, bright line to draw the shapes with.

Don't let the stitches get too long – they might pull out or get tangled in the next stitch!

Make three tiny stitches in the same place when you finish. Cut the thread off neatly.

Sideways stitch

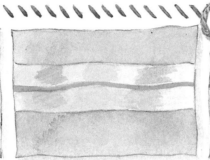

A sideways stitch is one half of a cross stitch. It looks pretty on its own, too.

Imagine two lines to fit the stitch between (or use some cloth with lines that you can follow).

Start each stitch on the bottom line and finish it on the top line just a little bit further on.

Cross stitch

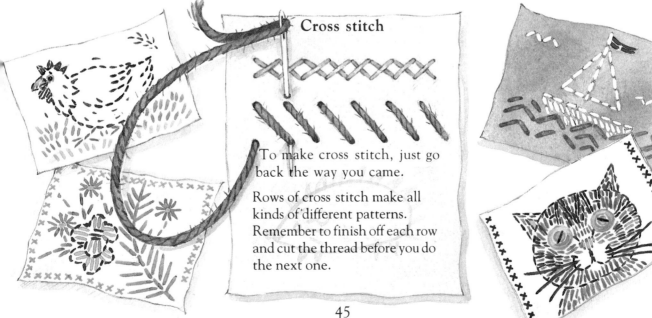

To make cross stitch, just go back the way you came.

Rows of cross stitch make all kinds of different patterns. Remember to finish off each row and cut the thread before you do the next one.

Big and little bags

Just fold some cloth and stitch it round
and here's what you can make:
a cover to put your comb in;
a purse to carry your money;
a small case for a mirror or glasses;
a big one for pencils or crayons;
a shoulder bag;
a shoe bag;
a toy bag;
a beach bag;
a laundry bag…

Running stitch

Push the needle
into the cloth and
out again a little
way along. Make
each stitch and gap
the same length.

Right and wrong side

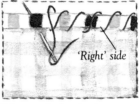

'Right' side

The right side is
usually more
brightly coloured
than the wrong side.

Making a pattern

You can draw round a book or packet. Make the pattern 1.5cm bigger all round than the size you want the bag to be.

If you fold the pattern, you can see how it works.

Put the pattern onto the cloth and pin it all the way round.

Cutting out

It's a good idea to kneel or stand at a table while you cut. Steady the cloth on the table (or the floor).

Joining up

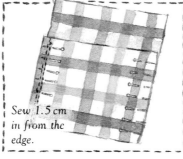

Sew 1.5 cm in from the edge.

Fold and pin the sides. Join them up with a neat running stitch. Then stitch back the way you came, filling in the gaps.

Turning under

Use running stitch along the fold.

Turn the bag inside out. For fabric that frays, fold the top edge over twice and pin it down. Stitch along the fold.

Button flap

Mark the spots for the button and buttonhole with chalk or pencil.

Fold the cloth to see where you want the button. Sew it on. Fold again to mark the spot for the buttonhole and snip there.

Cotton drawstring bag

Stop sewing one side about 2.5 cm from the top.

The right side of the fabric should face inwards.

Fold the fabric. Sew round two sides. Fold over the top edge twice and sew it down. Turn the bag right side out.

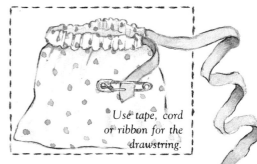

Use tape, cord or ribbon for the drawstring.

The turned-over bit makes a channel for a drawstring. Pin one end to the bag. Pin a safety pin to the other end. Push it through the channel.

a pocket doll

Pillows and cushions

It's easy to make a bag into a pillow. Just turn it and stuff it and sew up the opening. Use a plate or a biscuit tin as a pattern for a round cushion, or a box or magazine for a square-edged pillow. Here are some of the things that you can make.

a pillow-pet to travel with or sit on your bed for company

a Door no saur to keep the draughts out

a very thin scented pillow stuffed with lavender (use very tiny stitches so it won't leak)

What you need:

Materials

cloth

pins

newspaper

a pencil

scissors

needle and thread

Stuffing

cotton wool

old, clean stockings or tights

foam

rags cut into strips

Decoration

beads

sequins

wool

embroidery thread

bits of lace and ribbon

buttons

felt

Heart pattern cushion

1 Fold a piece of newspaper in half. Mark and cut out a shape like this using a plate for the curve. Then unfold it. It will be a heart-shape.

First fold the fabric or place two pieces together with the 'right' sides facing each other.

2 Pin the pattern onto the fabric. Cut out and sew all round with back stitch. Leave an opening (about 5cm) for turning and stuffing.

Make stitches small and neat.

3 Turn it right-side out, stuff it and close the opening with over stitching.

Door no saur...

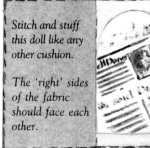
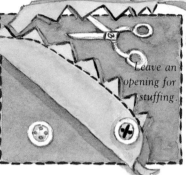

1 Fold a piece of hessian in half lengthways and pin it together. Sew a big seam for the spikes along its spine.

2 Before you stuff it, sew on the button eyes and add a felt tongue or a mouth or fangs. Cut out the spikes along its spine.

3 Poke stuffing all down its length, to make it as firm as possible. Then sew up the nose opening with over stitching.

Pocket Doll

Stitch and stuff this doll like any other cushion.

The 'right' sides of the fabric should face each other.

1 Fold a strip of cloth (about 30cm long and 12cm wide) in half. Pin a paper shape like this onto it.

2 To make button eyes, you must mark where they go and stitch them onto the right side before you stitch the sides.

3 You might like to stitch or glue some hands and feet on first, too. You can stick on woolly hair and collars and floppy felt feet with Copydex.

Dressing up

Do you like pretending you're
someone else – perhaps a witch or
a wizard, a clown, a pirate, a gypsy,
a fairy – or Superman?
Here are some tricks that you
might like to know.

Making a cloak

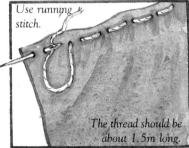

Use running stitch.

The thread should be about 1.5m long.

1 Use a towel, a piece of sheet
or even a tea towel. Thread a
big needle with a length of
strong button thread. Stitch
all along the top.

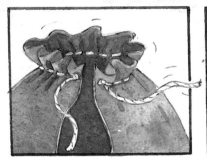

2 Pull the stitches to gather
up the cloth, until it's only as
wide as you want it. Make
three stitches in the same
place to hold it tight, and cut
the thread.

3 Sew on two bits of tape to
tie it with. You could then
glue, sew or paint on a big
red S for SUPERMAN!

Conical hats

card (or stiff paper)

scissors

sticky tape

paintbrush   paint

1 Get together all the things
shown above. Make a circle
on the card. Mark the
measurement you need in the
following way:

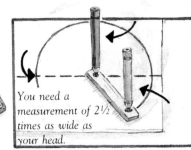

You need a
measurement of 2½
times as wide as
your head.

2 Punch holes at either end of
a strip of cardboard and stick
pencils through the holes.
Hold one pencil firm, swing
the other one around.

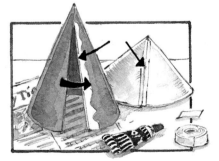

3 Cut the circle in half to
make a semi-circle. Roll it
into a cone and tape it.

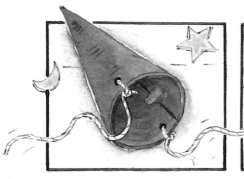  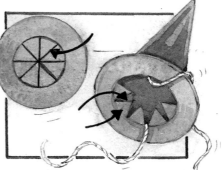

4 Punch little holes in the sides. Knot a piece of string, tape or shirring elastic, at each side to tie under your chin.

5 For a brim, use the circle-maker trick again. Then put the cone in the middle of the brim and draw around it.

6 Make little cuts to push out a hole in the middle. Bend these bits up inside the cone and tape them firmly.

Special effects

Some gold or silver paint is really magical, if you can get it, but thick coats of bright colours can look splendid, too. Try these:

Moon and stars to glue on the wizard's hat.

Magic wand – made from a cardboard star, glued to a stick.

Paper chain with cardboard star for a king or princess.

Crowns made from cardboard. (After painting, glue on jewels cut from glittery sweet papers.)

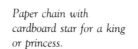

Egg-carton mask for an alien's eyeballs!

Curtain-ring earrings sewn on a scarf for a gypsy or pirate.

Medals – buttons glued or sewn to strips of ribbon, hung from a strip of card.

A good peg-leg for a pirate is a kitchen plunger. Make sure it's clean – ask someone before you use it. Bend your knee and tape it round – like this.

Corks, candle ends and string

Once you start noticing and collecting things,
you'll start to see a hundred ways to use them.
Corks for fishing floats and little boats –
and to stick on the tips of scissor blades to
keep them sharp.
String for tying parcels, carrying
bundles, pulling heavy things and
fencing a garden.
Candle ends for waxing the string
of the yoghurt pot telephone
line to help it carry the sound.

**Here are some
things you can do:**

Make a telephone
with yoghurt cartons.

Write secret messages with a
candle end. They'll show up
when you paint over them.

Fish for
minnows.

Hang up
paintings.

Useful knots

Someone who can tie a knot that doesn't come undone is a very handy person to have around. See if you can tie the knots shown here.

Small knot

This keeps the string from pulling through a little hole. You can thread beads to make necklaces and bracelets.

Timber Hitch

This is for holding things so you can carry them or drag them.

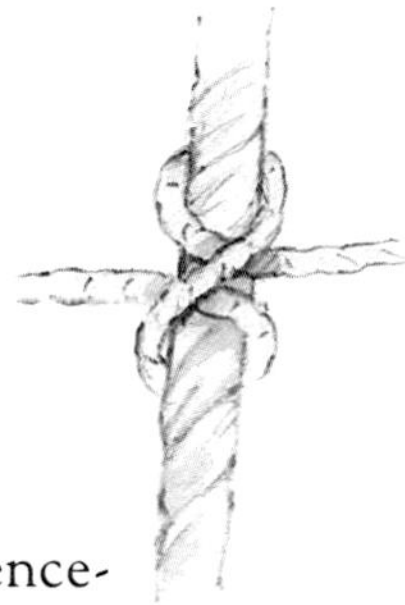

Clove Hitch

This will hold your fence-line to a stake or post.

Figure of 8 knot

This is a good knot for tying parcels.

Painting and decorating

Paint is really magical.
It can make an old kitchen chair or a
shabby doll's house look like new.
It can turn a funny old collection of tins
and jars into a matching desk set.
It can transform a stick into a magic
wand for a fairy godmother in a play –
a twig into a jewellery tree – a branch
into a snake – a pebble into a funny face
or a mysterious picture.

Here's what a painter needs:

Paint

Emulsion paint for big things,
poster paint for small things.
For a beautiful glossy paint, mix
powder paint with a PVA type glue.
(This will not be waterproof.)
For a varnish, use PVA or a
similar glue. Thin it with
water until you can brush it
on like paint.

Brushes

To paint something big,
such as a chair, you
need a good flat
bristle brush, at least
3cm wide. For smaller
things, you can use smaller
brushes.

wet
paint

Masking tape

To cover bits you don't
want the paint to touch.

Sandpaper

To smooth the surfaces
down before you paint. Ask
for fine or medium grade.

Use old jam-jars for
measuring and mixing and
for cleaning and storing
brushes. You also need
sticks to stir the paint
and some rags and newspaper
to keep things tidy.

Tips on painting

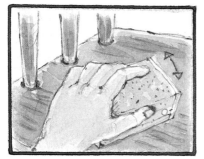

Big surfaces need to be smooth or the paint will flake. Rub them first with sandpaper. Wrap the sandpaper around a bit of wood and hold it down with drawing pins.

When the surface is perfectly smooth, wipe it with a damp cloth. Let it dry.

Dip your brush into the paint and then draw it against the inside rim of the tin to take extra paint off the brush. You don't want it to drip!

Wear an old shirt or apron and have a rag handy to wipe your hands on.

Spread newspapers down to catch any drips of paint.

The Pebble game

This is just to start your imagination working. Find three or four nice pebbles. Now look at one of the pebbles you have found. What is the very tiniest thing you could paint on it to make a picture?

If you add an eye – will it be a creature or a face? If you add a door – will it be a house?

If you add a sun – will it be a landscape…?

What do you think?

Building with bricks

With bricks and planks you can make real furniture.
You don't have to glue it. You don't have to nail it.
You just need to stack the bricks the way
a builder does.
Have you ever noticed how bricks
are laid in a wall? The top brick
presses down on the two
bricks under it holding them
in place. At the corners every
other brick goes sideways.
Look and see!

Here are some of the things you can do with them:

Two bricks make a book end.

You can buy bricks at a builder's merchant but, if you're lucky, you might find some lying about.

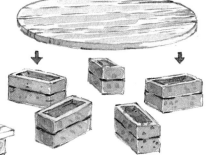

Two layers of five bricks each hold a round-top picnic table... or a grill for a barbecue.

Four bricks and a plank make a bench or a little seat.

Sixteen bricks and short plank make a desk. Use eight bricks for each side. Stack them cross-ways, like this.

Stacking shelves

A metre of space is all you
need for stacking shelves. To
make the shelves, you need:

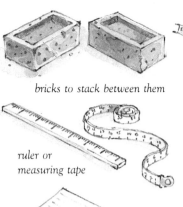

bricks to stack between them

*planks to fit the space –
use chipboard or
conti board, about
15mm thick*

*ruler or
measuring tape*

*pencil and
paper to write
down measurements*

1 Measure your widest book
to see how wide the shelf
should be.

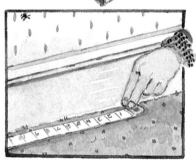

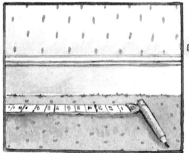

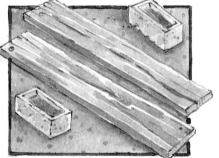

2 Measure along the wall to
see how long the shelf should
be. Hold down the starting
end of the tape or ruler and
note how far it stretches.

3 If it doesn't stretch far
enough, lay a pencil where it
ends and start again. Add
this extra bit to the number
at the end of the measure.

4 Now you can order planks
just the size you want.
Remember to count up how
many bricks you need.

5 Stack up the bricks and
boards and make your things
look beautiful.

Hammering practice

If you can hammer a nail straight and true there
are so many things that you can do…
Just think – a nail or two in a fence-post or a
tree-stump holds a dart board, a tent rope,
a washing line or a net for playing
ball games…

Here is how to practise:

*Use a soft
wood like
pine, or deal,
or chipboard.*

You might like to practise
first, with drawing pins.
You can push them in with
your thumb to get them
started.

Then practise aiming the
hammer to bang them in.

A mass of drawing pins
looks very rich and splendid.
You could make a glittery
book end or a paperweight
that looks like a tiny
treasure chest for a pirate.

Hammering a nail

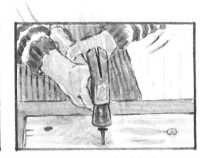

*Make sure the
wood is thick
enough so the
nail won't go
right
through it.*

1 To start, hold the nail in
place. Hold the hammer in
your other hand. Tap the
nail firmly but gently until
it stands up on its own.

2 Now you can hold the
hammer with both hands
and bang the nail firmly
into the wood.

3 If it starts to lean a bit,
give it a tap from the other
side to straighten it up.

Work on a worktable or something that won't be hurt if it gets dented.

Lay some newspapers down before you start, especially if you're working in the garden.

Afterwards, you can carefully tip the paper and any nails you've dropped will slide together so you can easily see and pick them up.

The papers should overlap.

Music-maker

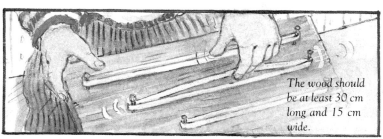

The wood should be at least 30 cm long and 15 cm wide.

You need a piece of wood, 3 or 4 rubber bands of different sizes and 2 nails to hold each rubber band stretched out. Stretch each rubber band, in turn, between your thumbs as far as it will go and have someone mark where your thumbs are on the wood. This is where the nails go.

Hoopla game

Big sticky tape rolls make perfect hoops when the sticky tape is gone. Save up two or three.

Colour some circles on a sheet of chipboard (at least 30cm square). Draw round a cup, a saucer and a plate to make the circles. Mark the score numbers. Hammer one long nail into each circle.

Leave room around each nail for a hoop to hang.

Key rack

Hammer nails into the wood to hang keys from.

Hang it with strips of ribbon or bias binding (sewing tape) held in place with drawing pins. Knot the ends tightly. Hang from 2 hooks or nails.

You need a starting line. Take it in turns to stand there and throw the hoops. Add up the scores to see who is the winner.

Setting up a workshop

You can have a workshop in a shoe box.
You can have a workshop on a shelf.
You can have it in the corner of
a cupboard.
It needs to be a place that's safe and
private where you can keep things
away from pets and very young children.

Here is how to set up a workshop:

You can make a set of matchbox drawers to keep little things in.

A big box is useful to store bits of wood and small boxes.

1 Hang or stand your tools where you can see them and easily reach for them. You need things such as scissors, hammer, brushes, ruler, pencils, stapler, sticky tape and glue.

2 Sort and separate the little things such as nails, drawing pins and paperclips. Keep them safe and close to hand in labelled jars and boxes.

3 Corks, rubber bands, chalk and bits of candle can go in jars. Keep string in a jar, rolled in a ball, so it's handy to get at. A big box is useful to store bits of wood and small boxes.

Matchbox drawers

Uhu or Copydex are especially good to use.

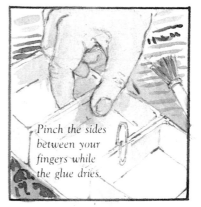

Pinch the sides between your fingers while the glue dries.

1 Glue them in a stack to make a tiny chest for paper fasteners, drawing pins or nails.

2 You can glue more stacks together for a wider set of drawers. Stick them on a base of card cut from a cereal packet.

3 A row of empty trays is good for sorting things. Stick them to a strip of card and glue the sides together.

Work on a sheet of newspaper or a tray – or keep a piece of oilcloth or PVC to be your work-top.

Sort tiny things on a paper so you won't lose them.

Keep a damp cloth handy to wipe your fingers, and wipe off extra glue before it hardens.

CHALK

61

BAKING

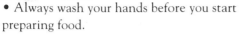

• Always wash your hands before you start preparing food.

• Wear an apron just in case you spill any food.

• Read the recipe very carefully before you begin.

• Make sure you have all the things you need before you start - and be sure to measure out the ingredients carefully.

• Always ask an adult to help you when you are cutting food or using an oven.

• If you're using a knife to cut food such as vegetables, always cut them on a chopping board and make sure the knife is sharp.

• When you're mixing ingredients in a bowl, stand it on a damp cloth to keep it from sliding about.

• Always use oven gloves on both hands when you're taking food out of a hot oven, or carrying hot plates and dishes.

• Keep your face away when you're opening the oven door to take food out - the steam is very hot.

• Keep pets out of the kitchen when you are cooking - they might get in your way or spread germs to the food.

• If you are going to use any electrical gadgets to help you cook, be careful not to touch the plugs with wet hands - you could get an electric shock.

• Leave the kitchen clean and tidy when you have finished with it.

GROWING

• If you're gardening, wear old clothes.

• Read seed packets carefully so you know how far apart the seeds should be - if seedlings grow too close together, they won't be strong. If this happens, you can pull out the smallest plants (this is called 'thinning out') but be careful not to hurt the stems and roots if you want to plant them somewhere else.

• Don't sow seeds on soil that is too cold and wet, they will just rot instead of growing.

• You can protect your seeds from birds and cats by covering them with netting.

• You can label your patches of seeds so you won't

forget what you've planted. Just put a little stick through a packet in two places (ask an adult to help you) and push it into the soil by the seeds.

• Your plants need plenty of water to grow, especially if they're in strong, direct sunlight, but don't water them too much or the roots will rot.

• Don't try to lift heavy rocks and stones, or tools such as spades, on your own - ask an adult to help you.

• Remember not to leave sharp tools such as garden forks lying around or you might cause an accident. Put everything away when you have finished your gardening for the day.

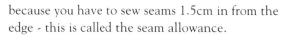

SEWING

- Get together everything you need before you start.

- Read the instructions carefully - perhaps two or three times to be sure you understand.

- Use sharp scissors to cut out fabric. Make sure you point them away from yourself - but be careful not to wave them around in the air as you might hurt somebody else.

- Cut the fabric carefully otherwise you will have to start again with a new piece of material.

- Don't forget that whatever you are making will always be smaller than the pattern. This is because you have to sew seams 1.5cm in from the edge - this is called the seam allowance.

- Work on the floor or a large table if you are cutting out material so that you can keep it straight and steady.

- Keep your pins and needles safely in containers. Don't leave them lying around when you have finished - someone might hurt themselves on them.

- Remember to tidy everything up when you have finished.

MAKING

- Make sure you have all the things you need near-to-hand before you start.

- Read the instructions carefully - as many times as you need to be sure you have understood everything.

- Wear an apron or put on old clothes, especially if you are going to be painting or using glue.

- Put down newspapers before you start - they will catch any drops of paint or glue. They will also make it easier to tidy up afterwards because bits of card or paper or pins will just fall onto the paper where you can see them.

- Always keep a damp cloth handy to wipe any spills of paint or glue off you or anything else straightaway - don't give them time to harden.

- Don't try to lift heavy things such as bricks or planks on your own - ask an adult to help you.

- When you're finding things to make something with or to paint, remember to check with an adult first to see if it is all right to use them.

- When you have finished, don't forget to tidy everything away. Wash your paintbrushes and be especially careful not to leave the lids off tins of paint or the tops off glue.

Index